P9-CFO-995

to

from

date

God's
Wisdom™
for
Mothers

Compiled by
Jack Countryman

God's Wisdom™ for Mothers
© 2011 by Jack Countryman

All rights reserved. No portion of this book may be
reproduced, stored in a retrieval system, or transmitted
in any form or by any means—electronic, mechanical,
photocopy, recording, scanning, or other—except for brief
quotations in critical reviews or articles, without the prior
written permission of the publisher.

Published in Nashville, Tennessee, by Thomas Nelson®.
Thomas Nelson is a registered trademark of Thomas
Nelson, Inc.

Cover design by Susan Browne Design, Brentwood,
Tennessee.

Thomas Nelson, Inc., titles may be purchased in bulk for
educational, business, fund-raising, or sales promotional
use. For information, please e-mail SpecialMarkets@
ThomasNelson.com.

Scripture quotations are taken from THE NEW KING
JAMES VERSION. © 1982 by Thomas Nelson, Inc. Used by
permission. All rights reserved.

ISBN-13: 9781404189560
ISBN-SE: 9781404189935

Printed in the United States of America
10 11 12 13 14 CP 6 5 4 3 2 1

Contents

God Walks with Mothers . . .

God Encourages Each Mother to . . .

God Teaches a Mother How to . . .

God Gives a Mother . . .

God's Wisdom . . .

God's Wisdom . . .
Is Needed in Every Mother's Life

Get wisdom! Get understanding!
   Do not forget, nor turn away from the
      words of my mouth.
Do not forsake her, and she will preserve you;
   Love her, and she will keep you.
Wisdom is the principal thing;
   Therefore get wisdom.
      And in all your getting, get understanding.
Exalt her, and she will promote you;
   She will bring you honor, when you
      embrace her.
She will place on your head an ornament
      of grace;
   A crown of glory she will deliver to you.
                              Proverbs 4:5–9

Let not mercy and truth forsake you;
Bind them around your neck,
Write them on the tablet of your heart,
And so find favor and high esteem
In the sight of God and man.

Proverbs 3:3–4

Wisdom has built her house,
She has hewn out her seven pillars;
She has slaughtered her meat,
She has mixed her wine,
She has also furnished her table.
She has sent out her maidens,
She cries out from the highest places of
the city,
"Whoever is simple, let him turn in here!"
As for him who lacks understanding,
she says to him,
"Come, eat of my bread
And drink of the wine I have mixed.
Forsake foolishness and live,
And go in the way of understanding."

Proverbs 9:1–6

Do not be wise in your own eyes;
　　Fear the LORD and depart from evil.
It will be health to your flesh,
　　And strength to your bones.

Proverbs 3:7–8

Walk in wisdom toward those who are outside, redeeming the time. Let your speech always be with grace, seasoned with salt, that you may know how you ought to answer each one.

Colossians 4:5–6

If any of you lacks wisdom, let him ask of God, who gives to all liberally and without reproach, and it will be given to him. But let him ask in faith, with no doubting, for he who doubts is like a wave of the sea driven and tossed by the wind.

James 1:5–6

You will keep him in perfect peace,
    Whose mind is stayed on You,
    Because he trusts in You.
Trust in the LORD forever,
    For in YAH, the LORD, is everlasting strength.

Isaiah 26:3–4

Unless the LORD builds the house,
    They labor in vain who build it;
    Unless the LORD guards the city,
    The watchman stays awake in vain.

Psalm 127:1

Incline your ear to wisdom,
    And apply your heart to understanding;
Yes, if you cry out for discernment,
    And lift up your voice for understanding,
If you seek her as silver,
    And search for her as for hidden treasures;
Then you will understand the fear of the LORD,
    And find knowledge of God.

Proverbs 2:2–5

God's Wisdom . . .
Is Essential to Cope with Life

For the LORD gives wisdom;
    From His mouth come knowledge and
        understanding;
He stores up sound wisdom for the upright;
    He is a shield to those who walk uprightly;
He guards the paths of justice,
    And preserves the way of His saints.
Then you will understand righteousness
        and justice,
    Equity and every good path.

Proverbs 2:6–9

Does not wisdom cry out,
    And understanding lift up her voice? . . .
"To you, O men, I call,
    And my voice is to the sons of men.
O you simple ones, understand prudence,
    And you fools, be of an understanding
        heart.
Listen, for I will speak of excellent things,
    And from the opening of my lips will
        come right things;
For my mouth will speak truth;
    Wickedness is an abomination to my lips.
All the words of my mouth are with
        righteousness;
    Nothing crooked or perverse is in them.
They are all plain to him who understands,
    And right to those who find knowledge.
Receive my instruction, and not silver,
    And knowledge rather than choice gold;
For wisdom is better than rubies,
    And all the things one may desire cannot
be compared with her."

Proverbs 8:1, 4–11

How much better to get wisdom than gold!
  And to get understanding is to be chosen
    rather than silver.

Proverbs 16:16

I, wisdom, dwell with prudence,
  And find out knowledge and discretion.
The fear of the LORD is to hate evil;
  Pride and arrogance and the evil way
  And the perverse mouth I hate.
Counsel is mine, and sound wisdom;
  I am understanding, I have strength.

Proverbs 8:12–14

For God gives wisdom and knowledge and
joy to a man who is good in His sight; but to
the sinner He gives the work of gathering and
collecting, that he may give to him who is good
before God. This also is vanity and grasping
for the wind.

Ecclesiastes 2:26

Let no one deceive himself. If anyone among you seems to be wise in this age, let him become a fool that he may become wise. For the wisdom of this world is foolishness with God. For it is written, "He catches the wise in their own craftiness"; and again, "The Lord knows the thoughts of the wise, that they are futile."

1 Corinthians 3:18–20

But the salvation of the righteous is from
    the Lord;
  He is their strength in the time of trouble.
And the Lord shall help them and
    deliver them;
  He shall deliver them from the wicked,
  And save them,
  Because they trust in Him.

Psalm 37:39–40

God's Wisdom . . .
Must Be Sought

When wisdom enters your heart,
    And knowledge is pleasant to your soul,
Discretion will preserve you;
    Understanding will keep you,
To deliver you from the way of evil.

Proverbs 2:10–12

Say to wisdom, "You are my sister,"
    And call understanding your nearest kin.

Proverbs 7:4

Through wisdom a house is built,
　　And by understanding it is established;
By knowledge the rooms are filled
　　With all precious and pleasant riches.

Proverbs 24:3–4

I love those who love me,
　　And those who seek me diligently will
　　　　find me.
Riches and honor are with me,
　　Enduring riches and righteousness.
My fruit is better than gold, yes, than fine gold,
　　And my revenue than choice silver.
I traverse the way of righteousness,
　　In the midst of the paths of justice,
That I may cause those who love me to
　　　　inherit wealth,
　　That I may fill their treasuries.

Proverbs 8:17–21

The heart of the righteous studies how
       to answer.

Proverbs 15:28

Let my mouth be filled with Your praise
    And with Your glory all the day.

Psalm 71: 8

O God, You are my God;
    Early will I seek You;
    My soul thirsts for You;
    My flesh longs for You
    In a dry and thirsty land
    Where there is no water.

Psalm 63:1

God's Wisdom . . .
Reaps Rewards

Happy is the man who finds wisdom,
　　And the man who gains understanding;
For her proceeds are better than the profits
　　　　of silver,
　　And her gain than fine gold.
She is more precious than rubies,
　　And all the things you may desire cannot
　　　　compare with her.
Length of days is in her right hand,
　　In her left hand riches and honor.
Her ways are ways of pleasantness,
　　And all her paths are peace.
She is a tree of life to those who take hold of her,
　　And happy are all who retain her.

Proverbs 3:13–18

Wisdom and knowledge will be the stability
of your times,
And the strength of salvation;
The fear of the LORD is His treasure.

Isaiah 33:6

Eat honey because it is good,
And the honeycomb which is sweet to
your taste;
So shall the knowledge of wisdom be to
your soul;
If you have found it, there is a prospect,
And your hope will not be cut off.

Proverbs 24:13–14

But seek first the kingdom of God and His
righteousness, and all these things shall be
added to you.

Matthew 6:33

Turn at my rebuke;
Surely I will pour out my spirit on you;
I will make my words known to you.

Proverbs 1:23

Now therefore, listen to me, my children,
For blessed are those who keep my ways.
Hear instruction and be wise,
And do not disdain it.
Blessed is the man who listens to me,
Watching daily at my gates,
Waiting at the posts of my doors.
For whoever finds me finds life,
And obtains favor from the LORD.

Proverbs 8:32–35

The hand of our God is upon all those for
good who seek Him.

Ezra 8:22

Come to Me, all you who labor and are heavy laden, and I will give you rest. Take My yoke upon you and learn from Me, for I am gentle and lowly in heart, and you will find rest for your souls. For My yoke is easy and My burden is light.

Matthew 11:28–30

Look to yourselves, that we do not lose those things we worked for, but that we may receive a full reward.

2 John 8

How sweet are Your words to my taste,
    Sweeter than honey to my mouth!
Through Your precepts I get understanding;
    Therefore I hate every false way.

Psalm 119:103–104

God's Wisdom . . .
Should Not Be Rejected

The simple inherit folly,
   But the prudent are crowned with knowledge.
                                   Proverbs 14:18

The heart of the prudent acquires knowledge,
   And the ear of the wise seeks knowledge.
                                   Proverbs 18:15

A fool despises his father's instruction,
   But he who receives correction is prudent.
                                   Proverbs 15:5

Houses and riches are an inheritance
      from fathers,
    But a prudent wife is from the LORD.

Proverbs 19:14

The wise in heart will be called prudent,
    And sweetness of the lips increases learning.

Proverbs 16:21

Wise people store up knowledge,
    But the mouth of the foolish is near
      destruction.

Proverbs 10:14

The Crown of an
Excellent Mother . . .

The Crown of an Excellent Mother . . .
Is of Great Value

Who can find a virtuous wife?
> For her worth is far above rubies.
>> *Proverbs 31:10*

She opens her mouth with wisdom,
> And on her tongue is the law of kindness.
She watches over the ways of her household,
> And does not eat the bread of idleness.
Her children rise up and call her blessed;
> Her husband also, and he praises her.
>> *Proverbs 31:26–28*

Charm is deceitful and beauty is passing,
But a woman who fears the LORD, she
shall be praised.
Give her of the fruit of her hands,
And let her own works praise her in
the gates.

Proverbs 31:30–31

The wise woman builds her house,
But the foolish pulls it down with
her hands.

Proverbs 14:1

The heart of her husband safely trusts her;
So he will have no lack of gain.
She does him good and not evil
All the days of her life.

Proverbs 31:11–12

The silver-haired head is a crown of glory,
If it is found in the way of righteousness.

Proverbs 16:31

She considers a field and buys it;
From her profits she plants a vineyard.

Proverbs 31:16

The Crown of an Excellent Mother . . .
Is from God

The LORD by wisdom founded the earth;
By understanding He established the heavens;
By His knowledge the depths were broken up,
And clouds drop down the dew.

Proverbs 3:19–20

Wisdom calls aloud outside;
She raises her voice in the open squares.
She cries out in the chief concourses,
At the openings of the gates in the city
She speaks her words.

Proverbs 1:20–21

The LORD possessed me at the beginning of
     His way,
     Before His works of old.
I have been established from everlasting,
     From the beginning, before there was
          ever an earth.
When there were no depths I was brought
          forth,
     When there were no fountains abounding
          with water.
Before the mountains were settled,
     Before the hills, I was brought forth;
While as yet He had not made the earth or
          the fields,
     Or the primal dust of the world.
When He prepared the heavens, I was there,
     When He drew a circle on the face of
          the deep,
When He established the clouds above,
     When He strengthened the fountains of
          the deep,
When He assigned to the sea its limit,
     So that the waters would not transgress
          His command,

When He marked out the foundations of
    the earth,
Then I was beside Him as a master craftsman;
    And I was daily His delight,
    Rejoicing always before Him,
Rejoicing in His inhabited world,
    And my delight was with the sons of men.

Proverbs 8:22–31

I am the vine, you are the branches. He who
abides in Me, and I in him, bears much fruit;
for without Me you can do nothing. . . . You
did not choose Me, but I chose you and
appointed you that you should go and bear
fruit, and that your fruit should remain, that
whatever you ask the Father in My name He
may give you.

John 15:5, 16

I will instruct you and teach you in the way
        you should go;
    I will guide you with My eye.

Psalm 32:8

The LORD will guide you continually,
    And satisfy your soul in drought,
    And strengthen your bones;
    You shall be like a watered garden,
    And like a spring of water, whose
        waters do not fail.

Isaiah 58:11

[God] only is my rock and my salvation;
    He is my defense;
    I shall not be moved.
In God is my salvation and my glory;
    The rock of my strength,
    And my refuge, is in God.

Psalm 62:6–7

The Crown of an
Excellent Mother . . .
Reveals Character Above Reproach

I, wisdom, dwell with prudence,
    And find out knowledge and discretion.
The fear of the LORD is to hate evil;
    Pride and arrogance and the evil way
    And the perverse mouth I hate.
Counsel is mine, and sound wisdom;
    I am understanding, I have strength.

Proverbs 8:12–14

The words of a man's mouth are deep waters;
    The wellspring of wisdom is a flowing brook

Proverbs 18:4

Now therefore, listen to me, my children,
  For blessed are those who keep my ways.
Hear instruction and be wise,
  And do not disdain it.
Blessed is the man who listens to me,
  Watching daily at my gates,
  Waiting at the posts of my doors.
For whoever finds me finds life,
  And obtains favor from the LORD;
But he who sins against me wrongs his
    own soul;
  All those who hate me love death.

Proverbs 8:32–36

Who is the man that fears the LORD?
  Him shall He teach in the way He chooses.
He himself shall dwell in prosperity,
  And his descendants shall inherit
    the earth.

Psalm 25:12–13

He who gets wisdom loves his own soul;
　　He who keeps understanding will find
　　　　good.

Proverbs 19:8

Hear . . . and receive my sayings,
　　And the years of your life will be many.
I have taught you in the way of wisdom;
　　I have led you in right paths.
When you walk, your steps will not
　　　　be hindered,
　　And when you run, you will not stumble.
Take firm hold of instruction, do not let go;
　　Keep her, for she is your life.

Proverbs 4:10–13

An excellent wife is the crown of her husband.

Proverbs 12:4

The Crown of an Excellent Mother . . .
Is Morally Upright

A foolish woman is clamorous;
>She is simple, and knows nothing.
For she sits at the door of her house,
>On a seat by the highest places of the city,
To call to those who pass by,
>Who go straight on their way:
"Whoever is simple, let him turn in here";
>And as for him who lacks understanding,
>>she says to him,
"Stolen water is sweet,
>And bread eaten in secret is pleasant."
But he does not know that the dead are there,
>That her guests are in the depths of hell.
>>>>*Proverbs 9:13–18*

Say to wisdom, "You are my sister,"
    And call understanding your nearest kin.
                        Proverbs 7:4

The fear of the L ORD leads to life,
    And he who has it will abide in
        satisfaction;
    He will not be visited with evil.
                        Proverbs 19:23

A gracious woman retains honor,
    But ruthless men retain riches.
                        Proverbs 11:16

Charm is deceitful and beauty is passing,
    But a woman who fears the L ORD, she
        shall be praised.
                        Proverbs 31:30

When wisdom enters your heart,
And knowledge is pleasant to your soul,
Discretion will preserve you;
Understanding will keep you,
To deliver you from the way of evil,
From the man who speaks perverse things,
From those who leave the paths of uprightness
To walk in the ways of darkness;
Who rejoice in doing evil,
And delight in the perversity of the
wicked;
Whose ways are crooked,
And who are devious in their paths—
So you may walk in the way of goodness,
And keep to the paths of righteousness.
For the upright will dwell in the land,
And the blameless will remain in it;
But the wicked will be cut off from the earth,
And the unfaithful will be uprooted from it.

Proverbs 2:10–15, 20–22

She extends her hand to the poor,
    Yes, she reaches out her hands to
      the needy.

Proverbs 31:20

The Crown of an
Excellent Mother . . .
Honors Her Husband

The heart of her husband safely trusts her;
    So he will have no lack of gain.
She does him good and not evil
    All the days of her life.

Proverbs 31:11–12

Wives, submit to your own husbands, as to
the Lord. For the husband is head of the wife,
as also Christ is head of the church; and He is
the Savior of the body. Therefore, just as the
church is subject to Christ, so let the wives be
to their own husbands in everything.

Ephesians 5:22–24

Nevertheless let each one of you in particular
so love his own wife as himself, and let the wife
see that she respects her husband.

Ephesians 5:33

Her husband is known in the gates,
   When he sits among the elders of the land.

Proverbs 31:23

Wives, likewise, be submissive to your own
husbands, that even if some do not obey the
word, they, without a word, may be won by the
conduct of their wives.

1 Peter 3:1

The older women likewise, that they be
reverent in behavior, not slanderers, not given
to much wine, teachers of good things—that
they admonish the young women to love their
husbands, to love their children.

Titus 2:3–4

The Crown of an Excellent Mother . . .
Blesses Her Children

Her children rise up and call her blessed.

Proverbs 31:28

Train up a child in the way he should go,
   And when he is old he will not depart
      from it.

Proverbs 22:6

Even a child is known by his deeds,
   Whether what he does is pure and right.

Proverbs 20:11

O you afflicted one,
>Tossed with tempest, and not comforted,
>Behold, I will lay your stones with
>>colorful gems,
>And lay your foundations with sapphires.
I will make your pinnacles of rubies,
>Your gates of crystal,
>And all your walls of precious stones.
All your children shall be taught by the LORD,
>And great shall be the peace of your children.
>>*Isaiah 54:11–13*

Correct your son, and he will give you rest;
>Yes, he will give delight to your soul.
>>*Proverbs 29:17*

Behold, children are a heritage from the LORD,
>The fruit of the womb is a reward.
Like arrows in the hand of a warrior,
>So are the children of one's youth.
>>*Psalm 127:3–4*

The Crown of an Excellent Mother . . .
Displays Her Faithfulness

But you, beloved, building yourselves up on your most holy faith, praying in the Holy Spirit, keep yourselves in the love of God, looking for the mercy of our Lord Jesus Christ unto eternal life.

Jude 20–21

It is good to give thanks to the LORD,
And to sing praises to Your name,
O Most High;
To declare Your lovingkindness in the morning,
And Your faithfulness every night.

Psalm 92:1–2

Blessed are the people who know the joyful
	sound!
	They walk, O Lord, in the light of Your
		countenance.
In Your name they rejoice all day long,
	And in Your righteousness they are
		exalted.
For You are the glory of their strength,
	And in Your favor our horn is exalted.

Psalm 89:15–17

But the fruit of the Spirit is love, joy, peace,
longsuffering, kindness, goodness, faithfulness,
gentleness, self-control. Against such there is
no law.

Galatians 5:22–23

Who is wise and understanding among you?
Let him show by good conduct that his words
are done in the meekness of wisdom.

James 3:13

I will sing of the mercies of the LORD forever;
With my mouth will I make known Your
faithfulness to all generations.
For I have said, "Mercy shall be built
up forever;
Your faithfulness You shall establish in the
very heavens."

Psalm 89:1–2

Forever, O LORD,
Your word is settled in heaven.
Your faithfulness endures to all generations;
You established the earth, and it abides.
They continue this day according to Your
ordinances,
For all are Your servants.

Psalm 119:89–91

Oh, love the LORD, all you His saints!
For the LORD preserves the faithful.

Psalm 31:23

The Crown of an Excellent Mother . . .
Holds Marital Fidelity Sacred

The righteousness of the upright will
     deliver them,
    But the unfaithful will be caught by
     their lust.

Proverbs 11:6

Therefore a man shall leave his father and
mother and be joined to his wife, and they
shall become one flesh.

Genesis 2:24

Many daughters have done well,
But you excel them all.

Proverbs 31:29

She opens her mouth with wisdom,
And on her tongue is the law of kindness.

Proverbs 31:26

The thoughts of the wicked are an
abomination to the LORD,
But the words of the pure are pleasant.

Proverbs 15:26

Finally, brethren, whatever things are true,
whatever things are noble, whatever things are
just, whatever things are pure, whatever things
are lovely, whatever things are of good report,
if there is any virtue and if there is anything
praiseworthy—meditate on these things.

Philippians 4:8

Therefore, just as the church is subject
to Christ, so let the wives be to their own
husbands in everything.

Ephesians 5:24

Blessed are the pure in heart,
    For they shall see God.

Matthew 5:8

The Crown of an Excellent Mother . . .
Comes to God Daily in Prayer

I sought the LORD, and He heard me,
   And delivered me from all my fears.
They looked to Him and were radiant,
   And their faces were not ashamed.
This poor man cried out, and the LORD
      heard him,
   And saved him out of all his troubles.
The angel of the LORD encamps all around
      those who fear Him,
   And delivers them.

Psalm 34:4–7

Let love be without hypocrisy. Abhor what is evil. Cling to what is good. Be kindly affectionate to one another with brotherly love, in honor giving preference to one another; not lagging in diligence, fervent in spirit, serving the Lord; rejoicing in hope, patient in tribulation, continuing steadfastly in prayer.

Romans 12:9–12

Confess your trespasses to one another, and pray for one another, that you may be healed. The effective, fervent prayer of a righteous man avails much.

James 5:16

The LORD will command His lovingkindness
      in the daytime,
    And in the night His song shall be with me—
    A prayer to the God of my life.

Psalm 42:8

Blessed is he whose transgression is forgiven,
   Whose sin is covered....
I acknowledged my sin to You,
   And my iniquity I have not hidden.
   I said, "I will confess my transgressions
      to the LORD,"
   And You forgave the iniquity of my sin.

For this cause everyone who is godly shall
      pray to You
   In a time when You may be found;
   Surely in a flood of great waters
   They shall not come near him.
You are my hiding place;
   You shall preserve me from trouble;
   You shall surround me with songs of
      deliverance.

I will instruct you and teach you in the way
      you should go;
   I will guide you with My eye.

Psalm 32:1, 5–8

I will bless the LORD at all times;
> His praise shall continually be in my
> > mouth.

My soul shall make its boast in the LORD;
> The humble shall hear of it and be glad.

Oh, magnify the LORD with me,
> And let us exalt His name together.

> > > *Psalm 34:1–3*

O LORD my God, I cried out to You,
> And You healed me.

O LORD, You brought my soul up from the grave;
> You have kept me alive, that I should not
> > go down to the pit.

Sing praise to the LORD, you saints of His,
> And give thanks at the remembrance of
> > His holy name.

For His anger is but for a moment,
> His favor is for life;
> Weeping may endure for a night,
> But joy comes in the morning.

> > > *Psalm 30:2–5*

The Crown of an Excellent Mother . . .
Is Sensitive to the Holy Spirit

Trust in the LORD with all your heart,
    And lean not on your own understanding;
In all your ways acknowledge Him,
    And He shall direct your paths.

Proverbs 3:5–6

It is the Spirit who gives life; the flesh profits nothing. The words that I speak to you are spirit, and they are life.

John 6:63

Commit your works to the LORD,
   And your thoughts will be established.

Proverbs 16:3

For the Holy Spirit will teach you in that very
hour what you ought to say.

Luke 12:12

Listen, for I will speak of excellent things,
   And from the opening of my lips will
      come right things;
For my mouth will speak truth;
   Wickedness is an abomination to my lips.
All the words of my mouth are with
      righteousness;
   Nothing crooked or perverse is in them.
They are all plain to him who understands,
   And right to those who find knowledge.

Proverbs 8:6–9

If you love Me, keep My commandments. And I will pray the Father, and He will give you another Helper, that He may abide with you forever—the Spirit of truth, whom the world cannot receive, because it neither sees Him nor knows Him; but you know Him, for He dwells with you and will be in you. I will not leave you orphans; I will come to you.

John 14:15–18

But the Helper, the Holy Spirit, whom the Father will send in My name, He will teach you all things, and bring to your remembrance all things that I said to you. Peace I leave with you, My peace I give to you; not as the world gives do I give to you. Let not your heart be troubled, neither let it be afraid.

John 14:26–27

However, when He, the Spirit of truth, has come, He will guide you into all truth; for He will not speak on His own authority, but whatever He hears He will speak; and He will tell you things to come. He will glorify Me, for He will take of what is Mine and declare it to you.

John 16:13–14

God's Wisdom
with Children . . .

God's Wisdom with Children . . .
Requires Daily Instruction

The heart of the wise teaches his mouth,
    and adds learning to his lips.
Proverbs 16:23

Hear, my children, the instruction of a father,
    And give attention to know understanding;
For I give you good doctrine:
    Do not forsake my law. . . .
    "Let your heart retain my words;
    Keep my commands, and live."
Proverbs 4:1–2, 4

The fear of the LORD is the beginning of
wisdom,
And the knowledge of the Holy One
is understanding.

Proverbs 9:10

Foolishness is bound up in the heart of a child;
The rod of correction will drive it far
from him.

Proverbs 22:15

Preach the word! Be ready in season and out
of season. Convince, rebuke, exhort, with all
longsuffering and teaching.

2 Timothy 4:2

Chasten your son while there is hope,
And do not set your heart on his
destruction.

Proverbs 19:18

God's Wisdom with Children . . .
Begins in the Home

Therefore whoever hears these saying of Mine, and does them, I will liken him to a wise man who built his house on the rock.

Matthew 7:24

"If anyone loves Me, he will keep My word; and My Father will love him, and We will come to him and make Our home with him."

John 14:23

Train up a child in the way he should go,
    And when he is old he will not depart
        from it.

Proverbs 22:6

Jesus said, "Let the little children come to Me, and do not forbid them; for of such is the kingdom of heaven."

Matthew 19:14

And these words which I command you today shall be in your heart. You shall teach them diligently to your children, and shall talk of them when you sit in your house, when you walk by the way, when you lie down, and when you rise up.

Deuteronomy 6:6–7

He who spares his rod hates his son,
But he who loves him disciplines him
promptly.

Proverbs 13:24

Walk in wisdom toward those who are outside,
redeeming the time. Let your speech always be
with grace, seasoned with salt, that you may
know how you ought to answer each one.

Colossians 4:5–6

God's Wisdom with Children . . .

Includes Proper Training and Correction

Go to the ant . . .
    Consider her ways and be wise,
Which, having no captain,
    Overseer or ruler,
Provides her supplies in the summer,
    And gathers her food in the harvest.

Proverbs 6:6–11

Correct your son, and he will give you rest;
    Yes, he will give delight to your soul.

Proverbs 29:17

Do not despise the chastening of the LORD,
  Nor detest His correction;
For whom the LORD loves He corrects,
  Just as a father the son in whom he
    delights.

Proverbs 3:11–12

God's Wisdom with Children . . .
Reaps Lasting Rewards

Rejoice and be exceedingly glad, for great is your reward in heaven.

Matthew 5:12

But love your enemies, do good, and lend, hoping for nothing in return; and your reward will be great, and you will be sons of the Most High. For He is kind to the unthankful and evil. Therefore be merciful, just as your Father also is merciful.

Luke 6:35–36

Look to yourselves, that we do not lose those
things we worked for, but that we may receive
a full reward.

2 John 8

Now he who plants and he who waters are
one, and each one will receive his own reward
according to his own labor.

For we are God's fellow workers; you are
God's field, you are God's building.

1 Corinthians 3:8–9

For God so loved the world that He gave
His only begotten Son, that whoever
believes in Him should not perish but have
everlasting life.

John 3:16

The father of the righteous will greatly rejoice,
    And he who begets a wise child will
        delight in him.
Let your father and your mother be glad,
    And let her who bore you rejoice.

Proverbs 23:24–25

The fear of the Lord is a fountain of life.

Proverbs 14:27

Do not lose heart. . . . For our light affliction,
which is but for a moment, is working for us a
far more exceeding and eternal weight of glory.

2 Corinthians 4:16–17

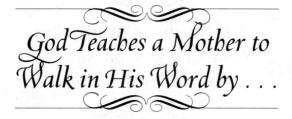

God Teaches a Mother to Walk in His Word by . . .

God Teaches a Mother to Walk in His Word by . . .
Praising His Holy Name

I will bless the LORD at all times;
    His praise shall continually be in my
        mouth.
My soul shall make its boast in the LORD;
    The humble shall hear of it and be glad.
Oh, magnify the LORD with me,
    And let us exalt His name together.
I sought the LORD, and He heard me,
    And delivered me from all my fears.

Psalm 34:1–4

So they rose early in the morning and went out into the Wilderness of Tekoa; and as they went out, Jehoshaphat stood and said, "Hear me, O Judah and you inhabitants of Jerusalem: Believe in the LORD your God, and you shall be established; believe His prophets, and you shall prosper." And when he had consulted with the people, he appointed those who should sing to the LORD, and who should praise the beauty of holiness, as they went out before the army and were saying:

"Praise the LORD,
For His mercy endures forever."

2 Chronicles 20:20–21

Charm is deceitful and beauty is passing,
But a woman who fears the LORD, she shall
be praised.
Give her of the fruit of her hands,
And let her own works praise her in
the gates.

Proverbs 31:30–31

Praise the LORD!
   Praise the LORD, O my soul!
While I live I will praise the LORD;
   I will sing praises to my God while I have
      my being.
Do not put your trust in princes,
   Nor in a son of man, in whom there is
      no help.
His spirit departs, he returns to his earth;
   In that very day his plans perish.
Happy is he who has the God of Jacob for
      his help,
   Whose hope is in the LORD his God,
Who made heaven and earth,
   The sea, and all that is in them;
   Who keeps truth forever,
Who executes justice for the oppressed,
   Who gives food to the hungry.
   The LORD gives freedom to the prisoners.

The LORD opens the eyes of the blind;
   The LORD raises those who are bowed
      down;
   The LORD loves the righteous.

The LORD watches over the strangers;
　　He relieves the fatherless and widow;
　　But the way of the wicked He turns
　　　　upside down.

The LORD shall reign forever—
　　Your God, O Zion, to all generations.
　　Praise the LORD!

Psalm 146

Let them shout for joy and be glad,
　　Who favor my righteous cause;
　　And let them say continually,
　　"Let the LORD be magnified,
　　Who has pleasure in the prosperity of
　　　　His servant."
And my tongue shall speak of Your
　　　　righteousness
　　And of Your praise all the day long.

Psalm 35:27–28

Whoever offers praise glorifies Me;
    And to him who orders his conduct aright
    I will show the salvation of God.

Psalm 50:23

Praise the LORD!
    Praise God in His sanctuary;
    Praise Him in His mighty firmament!
Praise Him for His mighty acts;
    Praise Him according to His excellent
        greatness!
Praise Him with the sound of the trumpet;
    Praise Him with the lute and harp!
Praise Him with the timbrel and dance;
    Praise Him with stringed instruments
        and flutes!
Praise Him with loud cymbals;
    Praise Him with clashing cymbals!
Let everything that has breath praise the LORD.
    Praise the LORD!

Psalm 150

God Teaches a Mother to Walk in His Word by . . .
Trusting in His Power

Trust in the LORD with all your heart,
    And lean not on your own understanding;
In all your ways acknowledge Him,
    And He shall direct your paths.

Proverbs 3:5–6

Lift up your eyes on high,
And see who has created these things,
Who brings out their host by number;
He calls them all by name,
By the greatness of His might
And the strength of His power.

Isaiah 40:26

As for God, His way is perfect;
    The word of the LORD is proven;
    He is a shield to all who trust in Him.

Psalm 18:30

In all things we commend ourselves as
ministers of God . . . by the Holy Spirit, by
sincere love, by the word of truth, by the power
of God, by the armor of righteousness on the
right hand and on the left.

2 Corinthians 6:4, 6–7

Whenever I am afraid,
    I will trust in You.
In God (I will praise His word),
    In God I have put my trust;
    I will not fear.
    What can flesh do to me?

Psalm 56:3–4

Great is our Lord, and mighty in power;
   His understanding is infinite.

Psalm 147:5

The LORD is my rock and my fortress and
      my deliverer;
   My God, my strength, in whom I
      will trust;
   My shield and the horn of my salvation,
      my stronghold.
I will call upon the LORD, who is worthy to
      be praised;
   So shall I be saved from my enemies.

Psalm 18:2–3

He gives power to the weak, and to those who
have no might He increases strength.

Isaiah 40:29

For God has not given us a spirit of fear, but of
power and of love and of a sound mind.

2 Timothy 1:7

In You, O Lord, I put my trust;
 Let me never be put to shame.
Deliver me in Your righteousness . . .
 Incline Your ear to me, and save me.
Be my strong refuge,
 To which I may resort continually;
 You have given the commandment to
save me,
 For You are my rock and my fortress.

Psalm 71:1–3

You will keep him in perfect peace,
 Whose mind is stayed on You,
 Because he trusts in You.
Trust in the Lord forever,
 For in Yah, the Lord, is everlasting strength.

Isaiah 26:3–4

God Teaches a Mother to Walk in His Word by . . .
Focusing on His Love

Who shall separate us from the love of Christ? Shall tribulation, or distress, or persecution, or famine, or nakedness, or peril, or sword? . . . I am persuaded that neither death nor life, nor angels nor principalities nor powers, nor things present nor things to come, nor height nor depth, nor any other created thing, shall be able to separate us from the love of God which is in Christ Jesus our Lord.

Romans 8:35, 38–39

You shall love the LORD your God with all your heart, with all your soul, and with all your strength. And these words which I command you today shall be in your heart. You shall teach them diligently to your children, and shall talk of them when you sit in your house, when you walk by the way, when you lie down, and when you rise up. You shall bind them as a sign on your hand, and they shall be as frontlets between your eyes.

Deuteronomy 6:5–8

Now by this we know that we know Him, if we keep His commandments. He who says, "I know Him," and does not keep His commandments, is a liar, and the truth is not in him. But whoever keeps His word, truly the love of God is perfected in him. By this we know that we are in Him. He who says he abides in Him ought himself also to walk just as He walked.

1 John 2:3–6

Oh, love the LORD, all you His saints!
　For the LORD preserves the faithful,
　And fully repays the proud person.
Be of good courage,
　And He shall strengthen your heart,
　All you who hope in the LORD.

Psalm 31:23–24

For this reason I bow my knees to the Father
of our Lord Jesus Christ, from whom the
whole family in heaven and earth is named,
that He would grant you, according to the
riches of His glory, to be strengthened with
might through His Spirit in the inner man,
that Christ may dwell in your hearts through
faith; that you, being rooted and grounded in
love, may be able to comprehend with all the
saints what is the width and length and depth
and height—to know the love of Christ which
passes knowledge; that you may be filled with
all the fullness of God.

Ephesians 3:14–19

If you love Me, keep My commandments. And I will pray the Father, and He will give you another Helper, that He may abide with you forever—the Spirit of truth, whom the world cannot receive, because it neither sees Him nor knows Him; but you know Him, for He dwells with you and will be in you. I will not leave you orphans; I will come to you.

John 14:15–18

As the Father loved Me, I also have loved you; abide in My love. If you keep My commandments, you will abide in My love, just as I have kept My Father's commandments and abide in His love.

These things I have spoken to you, that My joy may remain in you, and that your joy may be full.

John 15:9–11

God Teaches a Mother to Walk in His Word by . . .
Praying for His Will

Most assuredly, I say to you, he who hears My word and believes in Him who sent Me has everlasting life, and shall not come into judgment, but has passed from death into life. . . .

For as the Father has life in Himself, so He has granted the Son to have life in Himself, and has given Him authority to execute judgment also, because He is the Son of Man. . . .

I can of Myself do nothing. As I hear, I judge; and My judgment is righteous, because I do not seek My own will but the will of the Father who sent Me.

John 5:24, 26–27, 30

Deliver me, O Lord, from my enemies;
 In You I take shelter.
Teach me to do Your will,
 For You are my God;
 Your Spirit is good.
 Lead me in the land of uprightness.

Psalm 143:9–10

So He said to them, "When you pray, say:
 Our Father in heaven,
 Hallowed be Your name.
 Your kingdom come.
 Your will be done
 On earth as it is in heaven.
 Give us day by day our daily bread.
 And forgive us our sins,
 For we also forgive everyone who is
  indebted to us.
 And do not lead us into temptation,
 But deliver us from the evil one."

Luke 11:2–4

Is anyone among you suffering? Let him pray. Is anyone cheerful? Let him sing psalms. Is anyone among you sick? Let him call for the elders of the church, and let them pray over him, anointing him with oil in the name of the Lord. And the prayer of faith will save the sick, and the Lord will raise him up. And if he has committed sins, he will be forgiven. Confess your trespasses to one another, and pray for one another, that you may be healed. The effective, fervent prayer of a righteous man avails much.

James 5:13–16

See then that you walk circumspectly, not as fools but as wise, redeeming the time, because the days are evil.

Therefore do not be unwise, but understand what the will of the Lord is. . . . giving thanks always for all things to God the Father in the name of our Lord Jesus Christ.

Ephesians 5:15–17, 20

The LORD is far from the wicked,
But He hears the prayer of the righteous.

Proverbs 15:29

All that the Father gives Me will come to Me, and the one who comes to Me I will by no means cast out. For I have come down from heaven, not to do My own will, but the will of Him who sent Me. This is the will of the Father who sent Me, that of all He has given Me I should lose nothing, but should raise it up at the last day. And this is the will of Him who sent Me, that everyone who sees the Son and believes in Him may have everlasting life; and I will raise him up at the last day.

John 6:37–40

For this cause everyone who is godly shall pray
      to You
    In a time when You may be found;
    Surely in a flood of great waters
    They shall not come near him.
You are my hiding place;
    You shall preserve me from trouble;
    You shall surround me with songs of
      deliverance.

Psalm 32:6–7

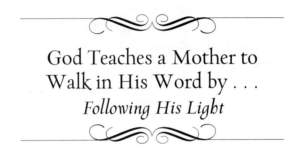

God Teaches a Mother to Walk in His Word by . . .
Following His Light

You are the light of the world. A city that is set on a hill cannot be hidden. Nor do they light a lamp and put it under a basket, but on a lampstand, and it gives light to all who are in the house. Let your light so shine before men, that they may see your good works and glorify your Father in heaven.

Matthew 5:14–16

I have come as a light into the world, that whoever believes in Me should not abide in darkness.

John 12:46

Oh, send out Your light and Your truth!
    Let them lead me;
    Let them bring me to Your holy hill
    And to Your tabernacle.
Then I will go to the altar of God,
    To God my exceeding joy;
    And on the harp I will praise You,
    O God, my God.

Psalm 43:3–4

Your word is a lamp to my feet
    And a light to my path.
I have sworn and confirmed
    That I will keep Your righteous judgments.
Psalm 119:105–106

For you were once darkness, but now you are
light in the Lord. Walk as children of light
(for the fruit of the Spirit is in all goodness,
righteousness, and truth).

Ephesians 5:8–9

The lamp of the body is the eye. Therefore, when your eye is good, your whole body also is full of light. But when your eye is bad, your body also is full of darkness. Therefore take heed that the light which is in you is not darkness. If then your whole body is full of light, having no part dark, the whole body will be full of light, as when the bright shining of a lamp gives you light.

Luke 11:34–36

This is the message which we have heard from Him and declare to you, that God is light and in Him is no darkness at all. If we say that we have fellowship with Him, and walk in darkness, we lie and do not practice the truth. But if we walk in the light as He is in the light, we have fellowship with one another, and the blood of Jesus Christ His Son cleanses us from all sin.

1 John 1:5–7

God Teaches a Mother to Walk in His Word by . . .
Rejoicing Day and Night

Rejoice in the LORD, O you righteous!
　　For praise from the upright is beautiful.
Praise the LORD with the harp;
　　Make melody to Him with an instrument
　　　　of ten strings.
Sing to Him a new song;
　　Play skillfully with a shout of joy.
For the word of the LORD is right,
　　And all His work is done in truth.
He loves righteousness and justice;
　　The earth is full of the goodness of
　　　　the LORD.

Psalm 33:1–5

But let the righteous be glad;
    Let them rejoice before God;
    Yes, let them rejoice exceedingly.
Sing to God, sing praises to His name;
    Extol Him who rides on the clouds,
    By His name YAH,
    And rejoice before Him.

Psalm 68:3–4

Oh, worship the LORD in the beauty of holiness!
    Tremble before Him, all the earth. . . .
Let the heavens rejoice, and let the earth be glad;
    Let the sea roar, and all its fullness;
Let the field be joyful, and all that is in it.
    Then all the trees of the woods will
        rejoice before the LORD.
For He is coming, for He is coming to judge
the earth.
    He shall judge the world with
        righteousness,
    And the peoples with His truth.

Psalm 96:9, 11–13

"Most assuredly, I say to you that you will weep and lament, but the world will rejoice; and you will be sorrowful, but your sorrow will be turned into joy. A woman, when she is in labor, has sorrow because her hour has come; but as soon as she has given birth to the child, she no longer remembers the anguish, for joy that a human being has been born into the world. Therefore you now have sorrow; but I will see you again and your heart will rejoice, and your joy no one will take from you."

John 16:20–22

Rejoice in the Lord always. Again I will say, rejoice!

Let your gentleness be known to all men. The Lord is at hand.

Philippians 4:4–5

Let love be without hypocrisy. Abhor what is evil. Cling to what is good. Be kindly affectionate to one another with brotherly love, in honor giving preference to one another; not lagging in diligence, fervent in spirit, serving the Lord; rejoicing in hope, patient in tribulation, continuing steadfastly in prayer; distributing to the needs of the saints, given to hospitality.

Bless those who persecute you; bless and do not curse. Rejoice with those who rejoice, and weep with those who weep. Be of the same mind toward one another. Do not set your mind on high things, but associate with the humble. Do not be wise in your own opinion.

Romans 12:9–16

Rejoice always, pray without ceasing, in everything give thanks; for this is the will of God in Christ Jesus for you.

1 Thessalonians 5:16–18

God Delights in
Mothers Who Are . . .

God Delights in
Mothers Who Are . . .
Seeking Him

Delight yourself also in the Lord,
　　And He shall give you the desires of
　　　　your heart.
Commit your way to the Lord,
　　Trust also in Him,
　　And He shall bring it to pass.

Psalm 37:4–5

I love those who love me,
　　And those who seek me diligently will
　　　　find me.

Proverbs 8:17

Seek the LORD while He may be found,
Call upon Him while He is near.
Let the wicked forsake his way,
And the unrighteous man his thoughts;
Let him return to the LORD,
And He will have mercy on him;
And to our God,
For He will abundantly pardon.

Isaiah 55:6–7

One thing I have desired of the LORD,
That will I seek:
That I may dwell in the house of the LORD
All the days of my life,
To behold the beauty of the LORD,
And to inquire in His temple.
For in the time of trouble
He shall hide me in His pavilion;
In the secret place of His tabernacle
He shall hide me;
He shall set me high upon a rock.

Psalm 27:4–5

Seek the LORD and His strength;
Seek His face evermore!

Psalm 105:4

For I know the thoughts that I think toward
you, says the LORD, thoughts of peace and not
of evil, to give you a future and a hope. Then
you will call upon Me and go and pray to Me,
and I will listen to you. And you will seek Me
and find Me, when you search for Me with all
your heart.

Jeremiah 29:11–13

Ask, and it will be given to you; seek, and you
will find; knock, and it will be opened to you. For
everyone who asks receives, and he who seeks
finds, and to him who knocks it will be opened.

Matthew 7:7–8

God Delights in Mothers Who Are . . .
Confident of Him

Grace and peace be multiplied to you in the knowledge of God and of Jesus our Lord, as His divine power has given to us all things that pertain to life and godliness, through the knowledge of Him who called us by glory and virtue, by which have been given to us exceedingly great and precious promises, that through these you may be partakers of the divine nature, having escaped the corruption that is in the world through lust.

2 Peter 1:2–4

Do not be afraid of sudden terror,
   Nor of trouble from the wicked when
      it comes;
For the Lᴏʀᴅ will be your confidence,
   And will keep your foot from being
      caught.

Proverbs 3:25–26

But the Lord is faithful, who will establish you and guard you from the evil one. And we have confidence in the Lord concerning you, both that you do and will do the things we command you. Now may the Lord direct your hearts into the love of God and into the patience of Christ.

2 Thessalonians 3:3–5

Therefore do not cast away your confidence, which has great reward. For you have need of endurance, so that after you have done the will of God, you may receive the promise.

Hebrews 10:35–36

Now this is the confidence that we have in Him, that if we ask anything according to His will, He hears us. And if we know that He hears us, whatever we ask, we know that we have the petitions that we have asked of Him.

1 John 5:14–15

I have fought the good fight, I have finished the race, I have kept the faith. Finally, there is laid up for me the crown of righteousness, which the Lord, the righteous Judge, will give to me on that Day, and not to me only but also to all who have loved His appearing.

2 Timothy 4:7–8

Christ [is the] Son over His own house, whose house we are if we hold fast the confidence and the rejoicing of the hope firm to the end.

Hebrews 3:6

In You, O Lord, I put my trust;
    Let me never be put to shame.
Deliver me in Your righteousness, and cause
        me to escape;
    Incline Your ear to me, and save me. . . .
For You are my hope, O Lord God;
    You are my trust from my youth.

Psalm 71:1–2, 5

God Delights in
Mothers Who Are . . .
Forgiven by Him

There is therefore now no condemnation to those who are in Christ Jesus, who do not walk according to the flesh, but according to the Spirit. For the law of the Spirit of life in Christ Jesus has made me free from the law of sin and death.

Romans 8:1–2

In Him we have redemption through His blood, the forgiveness of sins, according to the riches of His grace which He made to abound toward us in all wisdom and prudence

Ephesians 1:7–8

If we say that we have no sin, we deceive ourselves, and the truth is not in us. If we confess our sins, He is faithful and just to forgive us our sins and to cleanse us from all unrighteousness.

1 John 1:8–9

For as the heavens are high above the earth,
    So great is His mercy toward those who
        fear Him;
As far as the east is from the west,
    So far has He removed our transgressions
        from us.

Psalm 103:11–12

If My people who are called by My name will humble themselves, and pray and seek My face, and turn from their wicked ways, then I will hear from heaven, and will forgive their sin and heal their land.

2 Chronicles 7:14

In Him you were also circumcised with the circumcision made without hands, by putting off the body of the sins of the flesh, by the circumcision of Christ. . . .

And you, being dead in your trespasses and the uncircumcision of your flesh, He has made alive together with Him, having forgiven you all trespasses, having wiped out the handwriting of requirements that was against us, which was contrary to us. And He has taken it out of the way, having nailed it to the cross.

Colossians 2:11, 13–14

He has delivered us from the power of darkness and conveyed us into the kingdom of the Son of His love, in whom we have redemption through His blood, the forgiveness of sins.

Colossians 1:13–14

Now to Him who is able to keep you from
stumbling,
And to present you faultless
Before the presence of His glory with
exceeding joy,
To God our Savior,
Who alone is wise,
Be glory and majesty,
Dominion and power,
Both now and forever.
Amen.

Jude 24, 25

God Delights in Mothers Who Are . . .

Growing in Him

I will instruct you and teach you in the way
you should go;
I will guide you with My eye.

Psalm 32:8

Therefore lay aside all filthiness and overflow
of wickedness, and receive with meekness
the implanted word, which is able to save
your souls. But be doers of the word, and not
hearers only, deceiving yourselves.

James 1:21–22

We should no longer be children, tossed to and fro and carried about with every wind of doctrine, by the trickery of men, in the cunning craftiness of deceitful plotting, but, speaking the truth in love, may grow up in all things into Him who is the head—Christ.

Ephesians 4:14–15

Abide in Me, and I in you. As the branch cannot bear fruit of itself, unless it abides in the vine, neither can you, unless you abide in Me.

I am the vine, you are the branches. He who abides in Me, and I in him, bears much fruit; for without Me you can do nothing. . . .

If you abide in Me, and My words abide in you, you will ask what you desire, and it shall be done for you.

John 15:45, 7

O God, You are my God;
    Early will I seek You;
    My soul thirsts for You;
    My flesh longs for You
    In a dry and thirsty land
    Where there is no water.
So I have looked for You in the sanctuary,
    To see Your power and Your glory.
Because Your lovingkindness is better than life,
    My lips shall praise You.
Thus I will bless You while I live;
    I will lift up my hands in Your name.
My soul shall be satisfied as with marrow
        and fatness,
    And my mouth shall praise You with
        joyful lips.
When I remember You on my bed,
    I meditate on You in the night watches.
Because You have been my help,
    Therefore in the shadow of Your wings I
        will rejoice.
My soul follows close behind You;
    Your right hand upholds me.

Psalm 63:1–8

This Book of the Law shall not depart from your mouth, but you shall meditate in it day and night, that you may observe to do according to all that is written in it. For then you will make your way prosperous, and then you will have good success.

Joshua 1:8

You therefore, beloved, since you know this beforehand, beware lest you also fall from your own steadfastness, being led away with the error of the wicked; but grow in the grace and knowledge of our Lord and Savior Jesus Christ.

To Him be the glory both now and forever. Amen.

2 Peter 3:17–18

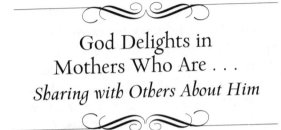

God Delights in
Mothers Who Are . . .
Sharing with Others About Him

What does it profit, my brethren, if someone
says he has faith but does not have works? Can
faith save him?

If a brother or sister is naked and destitute
of daily food, and one of you says to them,
"Depart in peace, be warmed and filled," but
you do not give them the things which are
needed for the body, what does it profit?
Thus also faith by itself, if it does not have
works, is dead.

James 2:14–17

This is He who came by water and blood—
Jesus Christ; not only by water, but by water
and blood. And it is the Spirit who bears
witness, because the Spirit is truth. For there
are three that bear witness in heaven: the
Father, the Word, and the Holy Spirit; and
these three are one. And there are three that
bear witness on earth: the Spirit, the water, and
the blood; and these three agree as one. If we
receive the witness of men, the witness of God
is greater; for this is the witness of God which
He has testified of His Son. He who believes
in the Son of God has the witness in himself;
he who does not believe God has made Him a
liar, because he has not believed the testimony
that God has given of His Son.

1 John 5:6–10

Revive me according to Your lovingkindness,
So that I may keep the testimony of
Your mouth.

Psalm 119:88

"[Jesus] committed no sin, nor was deceit found in His mouth"; who, when He was reviled, did not revile in return; when He suffered, He did not threaten, but committed Himself to Him who judges righteously.

1 Peter 2:22–23

Blessed are the undefiled in the way,
  Who walk in the law of the LORD!
Blessed are those who keep His testimonies,
  Who seek Him with the whole heart!

Psalm 119:1–2

By this we know that we abide in Him, and He in us, because He has given us of His Spirit. And we have seen and testify that the Father has sent the Son as Savior of the world. Whoever confesses that Jesus is the Son of God, God abides in him, and he in God.

1 John 4:13–15

Teach me, O LORD, the way of Your statutes,
And I shall keep it to the end.
Give me understanding, and I shall keep
Your law;
Indeed, I shall observe it with my whole
heart.
Make me walk in the path of Your
commandments,
For I delight in it.
Incline my heart to Your testimonies,
And not to covetousness.
Turn away my eyes from looking at worthless
things,
And revive me in Your way.
Establish Your word to Your servant,
Who is devoted to fearing You.
Turn away my reproach which I dread,
For Your judgments are good.
Behold, I long for Your precepts;
Revive me in Your righteousness.

Psalm 119:33–40

God Walks
with Mothers . . .

God Walks with Mothers . . .
Through Heartache

Praise the LORD!
  For it is good to sing praises to our God;
  For it is pleasant, and praise is beautiful. . . .
He heals the brokenhearted
  And binds up their wounds.
He counts the number of the stars;
  He calls them all by name.
Great is our Lord, and mighty in power;
  His understanding is infinite.

Psalm 147:1, 3–5

Lord, You have heard the desire of the humble;
  You will prepare their heart;
  You will cause Your ear to hear,
To do justice to the fatherless and the oppressed,
  That the man of the earth may oppress
    no more.

Psalm 10:17–18

The righteous cry out, and the Lord hears,
  And delivers them out of all their troubles.
The Lord is near to those who have a broken
    heart,
  And saves such as have a contrite spirit.

Psalm 34:17–18

Come to Me, all you who labor and are heavy
laden, and I will give you rest. Take My yoke
upon you and learn from Me, for I am gentle
and lowly in heart, and you will find rest for
your souls.

Matthew 11:28–29

The LORD also will be a refuge for the oppressed,
    A refuge in times of trouble.
And those who know Your name will put their
        trust in You;
    For You, LORD, have not forsaken those
        who seek You.

Psalm 9:9–10

I will worship toward Your holy temple,
    And praise Your name
    For Your lovingkindness and Your truth;
    For You have magnified Your word above
        all Your name.
In the day when I cried out, You answered me,
    And made me bold with strength in
        my soul.

Psalm 138:2–3

The LORD will guide you continually,
And satisfy your soul in drought,
And strengthen your bones;
You shall be like a watered garden,
And like a spring of water, whose waters
do not fail.

Isaiah 58:11

The Spirit of the Lord GOD is upon Me,
Because the LORD has anointed Me
To preach good tidings to the poor;
He has sent Me to heal the brokenhearted,
To proclaim liberty to the captives,
And the opening of the prison to those
who are bound.

Isaiah 61:1

God Walks with Mothers . . .
Through Adversity

Blessed is the man whom You instruct,
    O Lord,
    And teach out of Your law,
That You may give him rest from the days
        of adversity,
    Until the pit is dug for the wicked.
                                Psalm 94:12–13

A merry heart does good, like medicine,
    But a broken spirit dries the bones.
                                Proverbs 17:22

If you faint in the day of adversity,
　　Your strength is small.

Proverbs 24:10

In the day of prosperity be joyful,
　　But in the day of adversity consider:
　　Surely God has appointed the one as well
　　　　as the other,
　　So that man can find out nothing that
　　　　will come after him.

Ecclesiastes 7:14

Beloved, do not think it strange concerning the
fiery trial which is to try you, as though some
strange thing happened to you; but rejoice
to the extent that you partake of Christ's
sufferings, that when His glory is revealed, you
may also be glad with exceeding joy.

1 Peter 4:12–13

Now thanks be to God who always leads us in triumph in Christ, and through us diffuses the fragrance of His knowledge in every place.

For we are to God the fragrance of Christ among those who are being saved and among those who are perishing.

2 Corinthians 2:14–15

Concerning this thing I pleaded with the Lord three times that it might depart from me. And He said to me, "My grace is sufficient for you, for My strength is made perfect in weakness." Therefore most gladly I will rather boast in my infirmities, that the power of Christ may rest upon me.

2 Corinthians 12:8–9

God Walks with Mothers . . .
Through Worry

My soul, wait silently for God alone,
   For my expectation is from Him.
He only is my rock and my salvation;
   He is my defense;
   I shall not be moved.
In God is my salvation and my glory;
   The rock of my strength,
   And my refuge, is in God.

Psalm 62:5–7

When you pass through the waters, I will
    be with you;
    And through the rivers, they shall not
        overflow you.
    When you walk through the fire, you
        shall not be burned,
    Nor shall the flame scorch you.
For I am the LORD your God,
    The Holy One of Israel, your Savior;
    I gave Egypt for your ransom,
    Ethiopia and Seba in your place.
Since you were precious in My sight,
    You have been honored,
    And I have loved you;
    Therefore I will give men for you,
    And people for your life.

Isaiah 43:2–4

Be anxious for nothing, but in everything by
prayer and supplication, with thanksgiving,
let your requests be made known to God;
and the peace of God, which surpasses all
understanding, will guard your hearts and
minds through Christ Jesus.

Philippians 4:6–7

I have called upon You, for You will hear me,
        O God;
    Incline Your ear to me, and hear
        my speech.
Show Your marvelous lovingkindness by
        Your right hand,
    O You who save those who trust in You
    From those who rise up against them.
Keep me as the apple of Your eye;
    Hide me under the shadow of Your wings.

Psalm 17:6–8

The LORD is high above all nations,
　　His glory above the heavens.
Who is like the LORD our God,
　　Who dwells on high,
Who humbles Himself to behold
　　The things that are in the heavens and
　　　　in the earth?
He raises the poor out of the dust,
　　And lifts the needy out of the ash heap,
That He may seat him with princes—
　　With the princes of His people.
He grants the barren woman a home,
　　Like a joyful mother of children.
Praise the LORD!

Psalm 113:4–9

Therefore I say to you, do not worry about
your life, what you will eat or what you will
drink; nor about your body, what you will put
on. Is not life more than food and the body
more than clothing? Look at the birds of the
air, for they neither sow nor reap nor gather

into barns; yet your heavenly Father feeds them. Are you not of more value than they? Which of you by worrying can add one cubit to his stature?

So why do you worry about clothing? Consider the lilies of the field, how they grow: they neither toil nor spin; and yet I say to you that even Solomon in all his glory was not arrayed like one of these. Now if God so clothes the grass of the field, which today is, and tomorrow is thrown into the oven, will He not much more clothe you, O you of little faith?

Therefore do not worry, saying, "What shall we eat?" or "What shall we drink?" or "What shall we wear?" For after all these things the Gentiles seek. For your heavenly Father knows that you need all these things. But seek first the kingdom of God and His righteousness, and all these things shall be added to you.

Matthew 6:25–33

God Walks with Mothers . . .
Through Impatience

For whatever things were written before were written for our learning, that we through the patience and comfort of the Scriptures might have hope. Now may the God of patience and comfort grant you to be like-minded toward one another, according to Christ Jesus, that you may with one mind and one mouth glorify the God and Father of our Lord Jesus Christ.

Romans 15:4–6

I wait for the LORD, my soul waits,
    And in His word I do hope.
My soul waits for the Lord
    More than those who watch for
        the morning—
    Yes, more than those who watch for
        the morning.

Psalm 130:5–6

Wait on the LORD;
    Be of good courage,
    And He shall strengthen your heart;
    Wait, I say, on the LORD!

Psalm 27:14

But those who wait on the LORD
    Shall renew their strength;
    They shall mount up with wings like eagles,
    They shall run and not be weary,
    They shall walk and not faint.

Isaiah 40:31

I cried to the Lord with my voice,
    And He heard me from His holy hill.
I lay down and slept;
    I awoke, for the LORD sustained me.

Psalm 3:4–5

My brethren, count it all joy when you fall into various trials, knowing that the testing of your faith produces patience. But let patience have its perfect work, that you may be perfect and complete, lacking nothing.

James 1:2–4

Therefore be patient, brethren, until the coming of the Lord. See how the farmer waits for the precious fruit of the earth, waiting patiently for it until it receives the early and latter rain. You also be patient. Establish your hearts, for the coming of the Lord is at hand.

James 5:7–8

God Walks with Mothers . . .
Through Disappointment

Pursue righteousness, godliness, faith, love, patience, gentleness. Fight the good fight of faith, lay hold on eternal life, to which you were also called and have confessed the good confession in the presence of many witnesses. I urge you in the sight of God who gives life to all things, and before Christ Jesus who witnessed the good confession before Pontius Pilate, that you keep this commandment without spot, blameless until our Lord Jesus Christ's appearing.

1 Timothy 6:11–14

LORD, I cry out to You;
    Make haste to me!
    Give ear to my voice when I cry out to You.
Let my prayer be set before You as incense,
    The lifting up of my hands as the
        evening sacrifice.

Psalm 141:1–2

Who is wise and understanding among you?
Let him show by good conduct that his works
are done in the meekness of wisdom. . . .

But the wisdom that is from above is
first pure, then peaceable, gentle, willing to
yield, full of mercy and good fruits, without
partiality and without hypocrisy. Now the fruit
of righteousness is sown in peace by those who
make peace.

James 3:13, 17–18

Therefore, brethren, stand fast and hold the traditions which you were taught, whether by word or our epistle. Now may our Lord Jesus Christ Himself, and our God and Father, who has loved us and given us everlasting consolation and good hope by grace, comfort your hearts and establish you in every good word and work.

2 Thessalonians 2:15–17

I know that whatever God does,
    It shall be forever.
    Nothing can be added to it,
    And nothing taken from it.
    God does it, that men should fear
        before Him.
That which is has already been,
    And what is to be has already been;
    And God requires an account of what
        is past.

Ecclesiastes 3:14–15

*God Encourages Each
Mother to . . .*

God Encourages Each
Mother to . . .
Cherish Her Family

Let brotherly love continue. Do not forget to
entertain strangers, for by so doing some have
unwittingly entertained angels. . . .

Let your conduct be without covetousness;
be content with such things as you have. For
He Himself has said, *"I will never leave you nor
forsake you."*

Hebrews 13:1–2, 5

Let all that you do be done with love.

1 Corinthians 16:14

This is My commandment, that you love one another as I have loved you. Greater love has no one than this, than to lay down one's life for his friends.

John 15:12–13

Our presentable parts have no need. But God composed the body, having given greater honor to that part which lacks it, that there should be no schism in the body, but that the members should have the same care for one another. And if one member suffers, all the members suffer with it; or if one member is honored, all the members rejoice with it.

1 Corinthians 12:24–26

For you, brethren, have been called to liberty; only do not use liberty as an opportunity for the flesh, but through love serve one another.

Galatians 5:13

Two are better than one,
>Because they have a good reward for
>>their labor.
For if they fall, one will lift up his companion.
>But woe to him who is alone when he falls,
>For he has no one to help him up.
Again, if two lie down together, they will
>>keep warm;
>But how can one be warm alone?

Ecclesiastes 4:9–11

As you do not know what is the way of the wind,
>Or how the bones grow in the womb of
>>her who is with child,
>So you do not know the works of God
>>who makes everything.
In the morning sow your seed,
>And in the evening do not withhold
>>your hand;
>For you do not know which will prosper,
>Either this or that,
>Or whether both alike will be good.

Ecclesiastes 11:5–6

God Encourages Each Mother to . . .
Give to Others with Grace

For he who sows to his flesh will of the flesh reap corruption, but he who sows to the Spirit will of the Spirit reap everlasting life. And let us not grow weary while doing good, for in due season we shall reap if we do not lose heart.

Galatians 6:8–9

She extends her hand to the poor,
 Yes, she reaches out her hands to
  the needy.

Proverbs 31:20

Give, and it will be given to you: good measure, pressed down, shaken together, and running over will be put into your bosom. For with the same measure that you use, it will be measured back to you.

Luke 6:38

Defend the poor and fatherless;
　　Do justice to the afflicted and needy.
Deliver the poor and needy;
　　Free them from the hand of the wicked.

Psalm 82:3–4

By this we know love, because He laid down His life for us. And we also ought to lay down our lives for the brethren. But whoever has this world's goods, and sees his brother in need, and shuts up his heart from him, how does the love of God abide in him?

　　My little children, let us not love in word or in tongue, but in deed and in truth.

1 John 3:16–18

He who receives you receives Me, and he who receives Me receives Him who sent Me. He who receives a prophet in the name of a prophet shall receive a prophet's reward. And he who receives a righteous man in the name of a righteous man shall receive a righteous man's reward. And whoever gives one of these little ones only a cup of cold water in the name of a disciple, assuredly, I say to you, he shall by no means lose his reward.

Matthew 10:40–42

Finally, all of you be of one mind, having compassion for one another; love as brothers, be tenderhearted, be courteous; not returning evil for evil or reviling for reviling, but on the contrary blessing, knowing that you were called to this, that you may inherit a blessing.

1 Peter 3:8–9

God Encourages Each Mother to . . .

Live a Life of Servanthood

Whoever desires to become great among you, let him be your servant. And whoever desires to be first among you, let him be your slave—just as the Son of Man did not come to be served, but to serve, and to give His life a ransom for many.

Matthew 20:26–28

For you, brethren, have been called to liberty; only do not use liberty as an opportunity for the flesh, but through love serve one another.

Galatians 5:13

As each one has received a gift, minister it to one another, as good stewards of the manifold grace of God. If anyone speaks, let him speak as the oracles of God. If anyone ministers, let him do it as with the ability which God supplies, that in all things God may be glorified through Jesus Christ, to whom belong the glory and the dominion forever and ever. Amen.

1 Peter 4:10–11

But Jesus called them to Himself and said to them, "You know that those who are considered rulers over the Gentiles lord it over them, and their great ones exercise authority over them. Yet it shall not be so among you; but whoever desires to become great among you shall be your servant. And whoever of you desires to be first shall be slave of all. For even the Son of Man did not come to be served, but to serve, and to give His life a ransom for many."

Mark 10:42–45

He who is faithful in what is least is faithful also in much; and he who is unjust in what is least is unjust also in much. Therefore if you have not been faithful in the unrighteous mammon, who will commit to your trust the true riches? And if you have not been faithful in what is another man's, who will give you what is your own?

No servant can serve two masters; for either he will hate the one and love the other, or else he will be loyal to the one and despise the other. You cannot serve God and mammon.

Luke 16:10–13

And whatever you do, do it heartily, as to the Lord and not to men, knowing that from the Lord you will receive the reward of the inheritance; for you serve the Lord Christ.

Colossians 3:23–24

Defend the poor and fatherless;
    Do justice to the afflicted and needy.
Deliver the poor and needy;
    Free them from the hand of the wicked.
They do not know, nor do they understand;
    They walk about in darkness;
    All the foundations of the earth are
unstable.

Psalm 82:3–5

God Encourages Each Mother to . . .
Pray for One Another

Call to Me, and I will answer you, and show you great and mighty things, which you do not know.

Jeremiah 33:3

And take the helmet of salvation, and the sword of the Spirit, which is the word of God; praying always with all prayer and supplication in the Spirit, being watchful to this end with all perseverance and supplication for all the saints.

Ephesians 6:17–18

Confess your trespasses to one another, and
pray for one another, that you may be healed.
The effective, fervent prayer of a righteous
man avails much.

James 5:16

Give ear, O Lord, to my prayer;
    And attend to the voice of my
supplications.
In the day of my trouble I will call upon You,
For You will answer me. . . .

Teach me Your way, O Lord;
    I will walk in Your truth;
    Unite my heart to fear Your name.
I will praise You, O Lord my God, with all
        my heart,
    And I will glorify Your name forevermore.
For great is Your mercy toward me,
    And You have delivered my soul from
        the depths of Sheol.

Psalm 86:6–7, 11–13

Now this is the confidence that we have in Him, that if we ask anything according to His will, He hears us. And if we know that He hears us, whatever we ask, we know that we have the petitions that we have asked of Him.

1 John 5:14–15

Come and hear, all you who fear God,
    And I will declare what He has done
        for my soul.
I cried to Him with my mouth,
    And He was extolled with my tongue.
If I regard iniquity in my heart,
    The Lord will not hear.
But certainly God has heard me;
    He has attended to the voice of my prayer.
Blessed be God,
    Who has not turned away my prayer,
    Nor His mercy from me!

Psalm 66:16–20

Sing to God, sing praises to His name;
    Extol Him who rides on the clouds,
    By His name YAH,
    And rejoice before Him.
A father of the fatherless, a defender of widows,
    Is God in His holy habitation.
God sets the solitary in families;
    He brings out those who are bound
        into prosperity;
    But the rebellious dwell in a dry land.

Psalm 68:4–6

Give ear to my words, O LORD,
    Consider my meditation.
Give heed to the voice of my cry,
    My King and my God,
    For to You I will pray.
My voice You shall hear in the morning,
      O LORD;
    In the morning I will direct *it* to You,
    And I will look up.

Psalm 5:1–3

I will praise You, O LORD, with my
        whole heart;
    I will tell of all Your marvelous works.
I will be glad and rejoice in You;
    I will sing praise to Your name,
        O Most High.
When my enemies turn back,
    They shall fall and perish at Your
        presence. . . .
The LORD also will be a refuge for
        the oppressed,
    A refuge in times of trouble.
And those who know Your name will put
        their trust in You;
    For You, LORD, have not forsaken those
        who seek You.

Psalm 9:1–3, 9–10

God Encourages Each Mother to . . .
Celebrate with Joy

I will praise You with my whole heart;
    Before the gods I will sing praises to You.
I will worship toward Your holy temple,
    And praise Your name
    For Your lovingkindness and Your truth;
    For You have magnified Your word
        above all Your name.
In the day when I cried out, You answered me,
    And made me bold with strength in
        my soul.

Psalm 138:1–3

O LORD, how manifold are Your works!
    In wisdom You have made them all.
    The earth is full of Your possessions—
This great and wide sea,
    In which are innumerable teeming things,
    Living things both small and great.
There the ships sail about;
    There is that Leviathan
    Which You have made to play there.
These all wait for You,
    That You may give them their food in
        due season.
What You give them they gather in;
    You open Your hand, they are filled
        with good. . . .
I will sing to the LORD as long as I live;
    I will sing praise to my God while I have
        my being.
May my meditation be sweet to Him;
    I will be glad in the LORD.

Psalm 104:24–28, 33–34

Oh, give thanks to the LORD!
    Call upon His name;
    Make known His deeds among the peoples!
Sing to Him, sing psalms to Him;
    Talk of all His wondrous works!
Glory in His holy name;
    Let the hearts of those rejoice who seek
        the LORD!
Seek the LORD and His strength;
    Seek His face evermore!
Remember His marvelous works which He
        has done,
    His wonders, and the judgments of
        His mouth.

Psalm 105:1–5

The LORD your God in your midst,
    The Mighty One, will save;
    He will rejoice over you with gladness,
    He will quiet you with His love,
    He will rejoice over you with singing.

Zephaniah 3:17

I will extol You, my God, O King;
    And I will bless Your name forever
        and ever.
Every day I will bless You,
    And I will praise Your name forever
        and ever.
Great is the LORD, and greatly to be praised;
    And His greatness *is* unsearchable.

One generation shall praise Your works
        to another,
    And shall declare Your mighty acts.
I will meditate on the glorious splendor
        of Your majesty,
    And on Your wondrous works.

Psalm 145:1–5

Now may the God of hope fill you with all joy
and peace in believing, that you may abound
in hope by the power of the Holy Spirit.

Romans 15:13

Happy is he who has the God of Jacob for
      his help,
  Whose hope is in the Lord his God,
Who made heaven and earth,
    The sea, and all that *is* in them;
    Who keeps truth forever,
Who executes justice for the oppressed,
    Who gives food to the hungry.
    The Lord gives freedom to the prisoners.

The Lord opens the eyes of the blind;
    The Lord raises those who are
      bowed down;
    The Lord loves the righteous.
The Lord watches over the strangers;
    He relieves the fatherless and widow;
    But the way of the wicked He turns
      upside down.

The Lord shall reign forever—
    Your God, O Zion, to all generations.
    Praise the Lord!

                      Psalm 146:5–10

Sing praise to the LORD, you saints of His,
    And give thanks at the remembrance
        of His holy name.
For His anger is but for a moment,
    His favor is for life;
    Weeping may endure for a night,
    But joy comes in the morning.

Psalm 30:4–5

As the Father loved Me, I also have loved
you; abide in My love. If you keep My
commandments, you will abide in My love,
just as I have kept My Father's commandments
and abide in His love.

    These things I have spoken to you, that My
joy may remain in you, and that your joy may
be full.

John 15:9–11

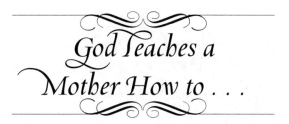

God Teaches a
Mother How to . . .

God Teaches a Mother How to . . .
Trust Him Completely

The LORD is your keeper;
    The LORD is your shade at your right hand.
The sun shall not strike you by day,
    Nor the moon by night.

The LORD shall preserve you from all evil;
    He shall preserve your soul.
The LORD shall preserve your going out
        and your coming in
    From this time forth, and even
forevermore.

Psalm 121:5–8

I will say of the LORD, "He is my refuge
      and my fortress;
   My God, in Him I will trust."

Surely He shall deliver you from the snare
      of the fowler
   And from the perilous pestilence.
He shall cover you with His feathers,
      And under His wings you shall take refuge;
      His truth shall be your shield and buckler.

Psalm 91:2–4

Incline your ear and hear the words of
      the wise,
   And apply your heart to my knowledge;
For it is a pleasant thing if you keep them
      within you;
   Let them all be fixed upon your lips,
So that your trust may be in the LORD;
   I have instructed you today, even you.

Proverbs 22:17–19

Trust in the LORD, and do good;
    Dwell in the land, and feed on
        His faithfulness.
Delight yourself also in the LORD,
    And He shall give you the desires of
        your heart.

Commit your way to the LORD,
    Trust also in Him,
    And He shall bring it to pass.
He shall bring forth your righteousness as
        the light,
    And your justice as the noonday.

Psalm 37:3–6

I will love You, O LORD, my strength.
The LORD is my rock and my fortress and
        my deliverer;
    My God, my strength, in whom I
        will trust;
    My shield and the horn of my salvation,
        my stronghold.

Psalm 18:1–2

But know that the LORD has set apart for
     Himself him who is godly;
  The LORD will hear when I call to Him.

Be angry, and do not sin.
     Meditate within your heart on your bed,
          and be still.
Offer the sacrifices of righteousness,
     And put your trust in the LORD.

Psalm 4:3–5

Trust in the LORD with all your heart,
     And lean not on your own understanding;
In all your ways acknowledge Him,
     And He shall direct your paths.

Proverbs 3:5–6

God Teaches a Mother How to . . .
Hold on to Her Faith

Therefore take up the whole armor of God, that you may be able to withstand in the evil day, and having done all, to stand.

Stand therefore, having girded your waist with truth, having put on the breastplate of righteousness, and having shod your feet with the preparation of the gospel of peace; above all, taking the shield of faith with which you will be able to quench all the fiery darts of the wicked one. And take the helmet of salvation, and the sword of the Spirit, which is the word of God.

Ephesians 6:13–17

Let us draw near with a true heart in full assurance of faith, having our hearts sprinkled from an evil conscience and our bodies washed with pure water. Let us hold fast the confession of our hope without wavering, for He who promised is faithful.

Hebrews 10:22–23

But without faith it is impossible to please Him, for he who comes to God must believe that He is, and that He is a rewarder of those who diligently seek Him.

Hebrews 11:6

Have I not commanded you? Be strong and of good courage; do not be afraid, nor be dismayed, for the LORD your God is with you wherever you go.

Joshua 1:9

Now He who has prepared us for this very thing is God, who also has given us the Spirit as a guarantee.

So we are always confident, knowing that while we are at home in the body we are absent from the Lord. For we walk by faith, not by sight.

2 Corinthians 5:5–7

Beloved, while I was very diligent to write to you concerning our common salvation, I found it necessary to write to you exhorting you to contend earnestly for the faith which was once for all delivered to the saints. . . .

But you, beloved, building yourselves up on your most holy faith, praying in the Holy Spirit, keep yourselves in the love of God, looking for the mercy of our Lord Jesus Christ unto eternal life.

Jude 3, 20–21

Therefore we also, since we are surrounded by so great a cloud of witnesses, let us lay aside every weight, and the sin which so easily ensnares us, and let us run with endurance the race that is set before us, looking unto Jesus, the author and finisher of our faith, who for the joy that was set before Him endured the cross, despising the shame, and has sat down at the right hand of the throne of God.

Hebrews 12:1–2

Therefore, my beloved brethren, be steadfast, immovable, always abounding in the work of the Lord, knowing that your labor is not in vain in the Lord.

1 Corinthians 15:58

God Teaches a Mother How to . . .
Live a God-Centered Life

For the grace of God that brings salvation has appeared to all men, teaching us that, denying ungodliness and worldly lusts, we should live soberly, righteously, and godly in the present age, looking for the blessed hope and glorious appearing of our great God and Savior Jesus Christ, who gave Himself for us, that He might redeem us from every lawless deed and purify for Himself His own special people, zealous for good works.

Titus 2:11–14

Create in me a clean heart, O God,
    And renew a steadfast spirit within me.
Do not cast me away from Your presence,
    And do not take Your Holy Spirit from me.

Restore to me the joy of Your salvation,
    And uphold me by Your generous Spirit.
Then I will teach transgressors Your ways,
    And sinners shall be converted to You.

Deliver me from the guilt of bloodshed,
        O God,
    The God of my salvation,
    And my tongue shall sing aloud of Your
        righteousness.

Psalm 51:10–14

I have been crucified with Christ; it is no longer I who live, but Christ lives in me; and the life which I now live in the flesh I live by faith in the Son of God, who loved me and gave Himself for me.

Galatians 2:20

Because Your lovingkindness *is* better than life,
     My lips shall praise You.
Thus I will bless You while I live;
     I will lift up my hands in Your name.
My soul shall be satisfied as with marrow
           and fatness,
     And my mouth shall praise You with
           joyful lips.

When I remember You on my bed,
     I meditate on You in the night watches.
Because You have been my help,
     Therefore in the shadow of Your wings
           I will rejoice.
My soul follows close behind You;
     Your right hand upholds me.

Psalm 63:3–8

The tongue of the wise uses knowledge rightly,
But the mouth of fools pours forth
foolishness.

The eyes of the LORD are in every place,
Keeping watch on the evil and the good.

A wholesome tongue is a tree of life,
But perverseness in it breaks the spirit.

Proverbs 15:2–4

Let the word of Christ dwell in you richly in all wisdom, teaching and admonishing one another in psalms and hymns and spiritual songs, singing with grace in your hearts to the Lord. And whatever you do in word or deed, do all in the name of the Lord Jesus, giving thanks to God the Father through Him.

Colossians 3:16–17

God Teaches a Mother How to . . .
Rest in His Protection

The LORD is your keeper;
    The LORD is your shade at your right hand.
The sun shall not strike you by day,
    Nor the moon by night.

The LORD shall preserve you from all evil;
    He shall preserve your soul.
The LORD shall preserve your going out and
        your coming in
    From this time forth, and even
        forevermore.

Psalm 121:5–8

Unless the LORD builds the house,
> They labor in vain who build it;
> Unless the LORD guards the city,
> The watchman stays awake in vain.
It is vain for you to rise up early,
> To sit up late,
> To eat the bread of sorrows;
> For so He gives His beloved sleep.

Behold, children are a heritage from the LORD,
> The fruit of the womb is a reward.
Like arrows in the hand of a warrior,
> So are the children of one's youth.
Happy is the man who has his quiver full
> of them;
> They shall not be ashamed,
> But shall speak with their enemies in
> the gate.

Psalm 127:1–5

But whoever listens to me will dwell safely,
> And will be secure, without fear of evil.

Proverbs 1:33

O LORD, You have searched me and known me.
You know my sitting down and my rising up;
    You understand my thought afar off.
You comprehend my path and my lying down,
    And are acquainted with all my ways.
For there is not a word on my tongue,
    But behold, O LORD, You know it altogether.
You have hedged me behind and before,
    And laid Your hand upon me.
Such knowledge is too wonderful for me;
    It is high, I cannot attain it.

Where can I go from Your Spirit?
    Or where can I flee from Your presence?
If I ascend into heaven, You are there;
    If I make my bed in hell, behold, You
        are there.
If I take the wings of the morning,
    And dwell in the uttermost parts of
        the sea,
Even there Your hand shall lead me,
    And Your right hand shall hold me.
If I say, "Surely the darkness shall fall on me,"
    Even the night shall be light about me;

Indeed, the darkness shall not hide from You,
    But the night shines as the day;
    The darkness and the light are both
        alike to You.

For You formed my inward parts;
    You covered me in my mother's womb.
I will praise You, for I am fearfully and
        wonderfully made;
    Marvelous are Your works,
    And that my soul knows very well.

Psalm 139:1–14

But know that the LORD has set apart for
        Himself him who is godly. . . .
    The LORD will hear when I call to Him.
You have put gladness in my heart,
    More than in the season that their grain
        and wine increased.
I will both lie down in peace, and sleep;
    For You alone, O LORD, make me dwell
        in safety.

Psalm 4:3, 7–8

But now, thus says the LORD, who created you,
   O Jacob,
   And He who formed you, O Israel:
   "Fear not, for I have redeemed you;
   I have called you by your name;
   You are Mine.
When you pass through the waters, I will be
   with you;
   And through the rivers, they shall not
   overflow you.
   When you walk through the fire, you
   shall not be burned,
   Nor shall the flame scorch you."
                                    Isaiah 43:1–2

But the Lord is faithful, who will establish you
and guard you from the evil one.
                              2 Thessalonians 3:3

God Teaches a Mother How to . . .
Obtain His Promises

For God is not unjust to forget your work and labor of love which you have shown toward His name, in that you have ministered to the saints, and do minister. And we desire that each one of you show the same diligence to the full assurance of hope until the end, that you do not become sluggish, but imitate those who through faith and patience inherit the promises.

Hebrews 6:10–12

Now this is the confidence that we have in Him, that if we ask anything according to His will, He hears us. And if we know that He hears us, whatever we ask, we know that we have the petitions that we have asked of Him.

1 John 5:14–15

By which have been given to us exceedingly great and precious promises, that through these you may be partakers of the divine nature, having escaped the corruption that is in the world through lust.

But also for this very reason, giving all diligence, add to your faith virtue, to virtue knowledge, to knowledge self-control, to self-control perseverance, to perseverance godliness, to godliness brotherly kindness, and to brotherly kindness love. For if these things are yours and abound, you will be neither barren nor unfruitful in the knowledge of our Lord Jesus Christ.

2 Peter 1:4–8

If you diligently heed the voice of the LORD
your God and do what is right in His sight,
give ear to His commandments and keep all
His statutes, I will put none of the diseases on
you which I have brought on the Egyptians.
For I am the LORD who heals you.

Exodus 15:26

For you are all sons of God through faith
in Christ Jesus. For as many of you as were
baptized into Christ have put on Christ. There
is neither Jew nor Greek, there is neither slave
nor free, there is neither male nor female; for
you are all one in Christ Jesus. And if you are
Christ's, then you are Abraham's seed, and
heirs according to the promise.

Galatians 3:26–29

Moreover he must have a good testimony among those who are outside, lest he fall into reproach and the snare of the devil.

Likewise deacons must be reverent, not double-tongued, not given to much wine, not greedy for money.

1 Timothy 3:7–8

The Lord is not slack concerning His promise, as some count slackness, but is longsuffering toward us, not willing that any should perish but that all should come to repentance.

2 Peter 3:9

God Teaches a Mother How to . . .
Cope with Change

Now this I say lest anyone should deceive you with persuasive words. For though I am absent in the flesh, yet I am with you in spirit, rejoicing to see your good order and the steadfastness of your faith in Christ.

As you therefore have received Christ Jesus the Lord, so walk in Him, rooted and built up in Him and established in the faith, as you have been taught, abounding in it with thanksgiving.

Colossians 2:4–7

Let love be without hypocrisy. Abhor what is evil. Cling to what is good. Be kindly affectionate to one another with brotherly love, in honor giving preference to one another; not lagging in diligence, fervent in spirit, serving the Lord; rejoicing in hope, patient in tribulation, continuing steadfastly in prayer; distributing to the needs of the saints, given to hospitality.

Bless those who persecute you; bless and do not curse. Rejoice with those who rejoice, and weep with those who weep. Be of the same mind toward one another. Do not set your mind on high things, but associate with the humble. Do not be wise in your own opinion.

Repay no one evil for evil. Have regard for good things in the sight of all men. If it is possible, as much as depends on you, live peaceably with all men.

Romans 12:9–18

Trust in the LORD with all your heart,
    And lean not on your own understanding;
In all your ways acknowledge Him,
    And He shall direct your paths.

Proverbs 3:5–6

I will bless the LORD who has given me counsel;
    My heart also instructs me in the
        night seasons.
I have set the LORD always before me;
    Because He is at my right hand I shall
        not be moved.

Therefore my heart is glad, and my
        glory rejoices;
    My flesh also will rest in hope. . . .

You will show me the path of life;
    In Your presence is fullness of joy;
    At Your right hand are pleasures
        forevermore.

Psalm 16:7–9, 11

For I know the thoughts that I think toward you, says the LORD, thoughts of peace and not of evil, to give you a future and a hope. Then you will call upon Me and go and pray to Me, and I will listen to you. And you will seek Me and find Me, when you search for Me with all your heart.

Jeremiah 29:11–13

As for God, His way is perfect;
    The word of the LORD is proven;
    He is a shield to all who trust in Him.

For who is God, except the LORD?
    And who is a rock, except our God?
It is God who arms me with strength,
    And makes my way perfect.

Psalm 18:30–32

God Teaches a Mother How to . . .

Rejoice in His Presence

Rejoice in the LORD, O you righteous!
 For praise from the upright is beautiful.
Praise the LORD with the harp;
 Make melody to Him with an instrument
 of ten strings.
Sing to Him a new song;
 Play skillfully with a shout of joy.

For the word of the LORD is right,
 And all His work is done in truth.
He loves righteousness and justice;
 The earth is full of the goodness of the LORD.

Psalm 33:1–5

O God, my heart is steadfast;
   I will sing and give praise, even with
      my glory.
Awake, lute and harp!
   I will awaken the dawn.
I will praise You, O Lord, among the peoples,
   And I will sing praises to You among
      the nations.
For Your mercy is great above the heavens,
   And Your truth reaches to the clouds.

Be exalted, O God, above the heavens,
   And Your glory above all the earth;
That Your beloved may be delivered,
   Save with Your right hand, and hear me.

Psalm 108:1–6

O God, You are more awesome than Your
      holy places.
   The God of Israel is He who gives strength
and power to His people.
   Blessed be God!

Psalm 68:35

When I remember You on my bed,
I meditate on You in the night watches.
Because You have been my help,
Therefore in the shadow of Your wings
I will rejoice.
My soul follows close behind You;
Your right hand upholds me.

Psalm 63:6–8

You who love the LORD, hate evil!
He preserves the souls of His saints;
He delivers them out of the hand of
the wicked.
Light is sown for the righteous,
And gladness for the upright in heart.
Rejoice in the LORD, you righteous,
And give thanks at the remembrance of
His holy name.

Psalm 97:10–12

What then shall we say to these things? If God is for us, who can be against us? He who did not spare His own Son, but delivered Him up for us all, how shall He not with Him also freely give us all things? Who shall bring a charge against God's elect? It is God who justifies. Who is he who condemns? It is Christ who died, and furthermore is also risen, who is even at the right hand of God, who also makes intercession for us. Who shall separate us from the love of Christ? Shall tribulation, or distress, or persecution, or famine, or nakedness, or peril, or sword? As it is written:

"For Your sake we are killed all day long;
We are accounted as sheep for the slaughter."

Yet in all these things we are more than conquerors through Him who loved us. For I am persuaded that neither death nor life, nor angels nor principalities nor powers, nor things present nor things to come, nor height nor depth, nor any other created thing, shall be able to separate us from the love of God which is in Christ Jesus our Lord.

Romans 8:31–39

I have set the LORD always before me;
   Because He is at my right hand I shall
      not be moved.
Therefore my heart is glad, and my
      glory rejoices;
   My flesh also will rest in hope.
For You will not leave my soul in Sheol,
   Nor will You allow Your Holy One to
      see corruption.
You will show me the path of life;
   In Your presence is fullness of joy;
   At Your right hand are pleasures
      forevermore.

Psalm 16:8–11

God Gives a Mother . . .

God Gives a Mother . . .
Hope for Eternal Life

But God, who is rich in mercy, because of His great love with which He loved us, even when we were dead in trespasses, made us alive together with Christ (by grace you have been saved), and raised us up together, and made us sit together in the heavenly places in Christ Jesus, that in the ages to come He might show the exceeding riches of His grace in His kindness toward us in Christ Jesus.

Ephesians 2:4–7

Sing to the LORD with thanksgiving;
    Sing praises on the harp to our God,
Who covers the heavens with clouds,
    Who prepares rain for the earth,
    Who makes grass to grow on the
        mountains.
He gives to the beast its food,
    And to the young ravens that cry.

He does not delight in the strength of
        the horse;
    He takes no pleasure in the legs of a man.
The LORD takes pleasure in those who
        fear Him,
    In those who hope in His mercy.

Praise the LORD, O Jerusalem!
    Praise your God, O Zion!
For He has strengthened the bars of your gates;
    He has blessed your children within you.

Psalm 147:7–13

For God did not appoint us to wrath, but
to obtain salvation through our Lord Jesus
Christ, who died for us, that whether we wake
or sleep, we should live together with Him.

Therefore comfort each other and edify
one another, just as you also are doing.

1 Thessalonians 5:9–11

If then you were raised with Christ, seek those
things which are above, where Christ is, sitting
at the right hand of God. Set your mind on
things above, not on things on the earth. For
you died, and your life is hidden with Christ
in God. When Christ who is our life appears,
then you also will appear with Him in glory.

Colossians 3:1–4

For as many as are led by the Spirit of God, these are sons of God. For you did not receive the spirit of bondage again to fear, but you received the Spirit of adoption by whom we cry out, "Abba, Father." The Spirit Himself bears witness with our spirit that we are children of God, and if children, then heirs—heirs of God and joint heirs with Christ, if indeed we suffer with Him, that we may also be glorified together. . . .

For we were saved in this hope, but hope that is seen is not hope; for why does one still hope for what he sees? But if we hope for what we do not see, we eagerly wait for it with perseverance.

Romans 8:14–17, 24–25

Blessed be the God and Father of our Lord
Jesus Christ, who according to His abundant
mercy has begotten us again to a living hope
through the resurrection of Jesus Christ from
the dead, to an inheritance incorruptible
and undefiled and that does not fade away,
reserved in heaven for you, who are kept by the
power of God through faith for salvation ready
to be revealed in the last time.

In this you greatly rejoice, though now
for a little while, if need be, you have been
grieved by various trials, that the genuineness
of your faith, being much more precious than
gold that perishes, though it is tested by fire,
may be found to praise, honor, and glory at
the revelation of Jesus Christ, whom having
not seen you love. Though now you do not
see Him, yet believing, you rejoice with joy
inexpressible and full of glory, receiving the
end of your faith—the salvation of your souls.

1 Peter 1:3–9

God Gives a Mother . . .
Wisdom for Daily Living

The days of our lives are seventy years;
And if by reason of strength they are
eighty years,
Yet their boast is only labor and sorrow;
For it is soon cut off, and we fly away.
Who knows the power of Your anger?
For as the fear of You, so is Your wrath.
So teach us to number our days,
That we may gain a heart of wisdom.

Psalm 90:10–12

The fear of the LORD is the beginning
        of wisdom;
    A good understanding have all those who
        do His commandments.
    His praise endures forever.

Psalm 111:10

How much better to get wisdom than gold!
    And to get understanding is to be chosen
        rather than silver.

Proverbs 16:16

Keep my commands and live,
    And my law as the apple of your eye.
Bind them on your fingers;
    Write them on the tablet of your heart.
Say to wisdom, "You are my sister,"
    And call understanding your nearest kin.

Proverbs 7:2–4

He who mistreats his father and chases away
his mother
Is a son who causes shame and brings
reproach.

Proverbs 19:26

Get wisdom! Get understanding!
Do not forget, nor turn away from the
words of my mouth.
Do not forsake her, and she will preserve you;
Love her, and she will keep you.
Wisdom is the principal thing;
Therefore get wisdom.
And in all your getting, get understanding.
Exalt her, and she will promote you;
She will bring you honor, when you
embrace her.
She will place on your head an ornament
of grace;
A crown of glory she will deliver to you.

Proverbs 4:5–9

Wisdom has built her house,
    She has hewn out her seven pillars;
She has slaughtered her meat,
    She has mixed her wine,
    She has also furnished her table.
She has sent out her maidens,
    She cries out from the highest places of
        the city,
"Whoever is simple, let him turn in here!"
    As for him who lacks understanding,
        she says to him,
"Come, eat of my bread
    And drink of the wine I have mixed.
Forsake foolishness and live,
    And go in the way of understanding."

Proverbs 9:1–6

But the wisdom that is from above is first pure, then peaceable, gentle, willing to yield, full of mercy and good fruits, without partiality and without hypocrisy.

James 3:17

God Gives a Mother . . .
Courage to Be a Woman of Integrity

Show me Your ways, O Lord;
    Teach me Your paths.
Lead me in Your truth and teach me,
    For You are the God of my salvation;
    On You I wait all the day. . . .
Keep my soul, and deliver me;
    Let me not be ashamed, for I put my trust
        in You.
Let integrity and uprightness preserve me,
    For I wait for You.

Psalm 25:4–5, 20–21

Blessed is the man
>> Who walks not in the counsel of the
>>>> ungodly,
>> Nor stands in the path of sinners,
>> Nor sits in the seat of the scornful;
But his delight is in the law of the LORD,
>> And in His law he meditates day and night.
He shall be like a tree
>> Planted by the rivers of water,
>> That brings forth its fruit in its season,
>> Whose leaf also shall not wither;
>> And whatever he does shall prosper.

The ungodly are not so,
>> But are like the chaff which the wind
>>>> drives away.
Therefore the ungodly shall not stand in
>>>> the judgment,
>> Nor sinners in the congregation of
>>>> the righteous.

For the LORD knows the way of the righteous,
>> But the way of the ungodly shall perish.

Psalm 1:1–6

I will sing of mercy and justice;
    To You, O LORD, I will sing praises.

I will behave wisely in a perfect way.
    Oh, when will You come to me?
    I will walk within my house with a
        perfect heart.

I will set nothing wicked before my eyes;
    I hate the work of those who fall away;
    It shall not cling to me.
A perverse heart shall depart from me;
    I will not know wickedness. . . .
    The one who has a haughty look and a
proud heart,
    Him I will not endure.

Psalm 101:1–5

Better is the poor who walks in his integrity
    Than one who is perverse in his lips, and
        is a fool.

Proverbs 19:1

Blessed are the undefiled in the way,
Who walk in the law of the LORD!
Blessed are those who keep His testimonies,
Who seek Him with the whole heart!
They also do no iniquity;
They walk in His ways.
You have commanded us
To keep Your precepts diligently.
Oh, that my ways were directed
To keep Your statutes!
Then I would not be ashamed,
When I look into all Your commandments.
I will praise You with uprightness of heart,
When I learn Your righteous judgments.
I will keep Your statutes;
Oh, do not forsake me utterly!

Psalm 119:1–8

The wise in heart will receive commands,
But a prating fool will fall.

He who walks with integrity walks securely,
But he who perverts his ways will
become known.

Proverbs 10:8–9

Dishonest scales are an abomination to
the LORD,
But a just weight is His delight.

When pride comes, then comes shame;
But with the humble is wisdom.

The integrity of the upright will guide them,
But the perversity of the unfaithful will
destroy them.

Proverbs 11:1–3